THE STAINED GLASS
COLORING BOOK

By Ruth Margaret Gallo Goliwas
and Dr. William H. Mackenzie Mackintosh

LITTLE SIMON

Published by Simon & Schuster Inc.

New York · London · Toronto · Sydney · Tokyo · Singapore

RUTH GLEANING BARLEY IN THE FIELDS

LOCATION: St. Giles' Cathedral, the High Kirk of Edinburgh
          Edinburgh, Scotland

INSTALLED: 1881

BIBLICAL REFERENCE: Ruth 2 and following

MAJOR COLORS: browns and pinks

JACOB OVERCOME AND BLESSED IN WRESTLING WITH THE ANGEL

LOCATION: The Cathedral Church of St. Mungo, Glasgow, Scotland
INSTALLED: 1859
BIBLICAL REFERENCE: Genesis 32 and following
MAJOR COLORS: blues and greens

MARY REIGNS AS THE BLESSED VIRGIN WITH THE CHRIST CHILD

LOCATION: Notre Dame Cathedral, Paris, France
INSTALLED: c. 1220
BIBLICAL REFERENCE: St. Luke 1: 46-48; 2: 21 and St. Matthew 1: 23
MAJOR COLORS: reds and blues

WISDOM—THE HIGHEST EXPRESSION OF THE HUMAN MIND

LOCATION: Laon Cathedral, Laon, France
INSTALLED: early 13th century
BIBLICAL REFERENCE: Proverbs 4: 5-12; St. Luke 11: 29-32; Psalm 111: 10
MAJOR COLORS: greens and blues

THE GOOD SAMARITAN HELPS A MAN ASSAULTED BY ROBBERS

LOCATION: Chartres Cathedral, Chartres, France
INSTALLED: early 13th century
BIBLICAL REFERENCE: St. Luke 10: 29-37
MAJOR COLORS: reds and blues

ADAM'S PUNISHMENT FOR DISOBEDIENCE—HE MUST WORK TO LIVE

LOCATION: Canterbury Cathedral, Canterbury, England
INSTALLED: 12th century
BIBLICAL REFERENCE: Genesis 3: 8-24
MAJOR COLORS: browns and purples

GOD IS PRAISED WITH MUSICAL INSTRUMENTS

LOCATION: Christ Church Cathedral, Oxford University,
          Oxford, England
INSTALLED: late 19th century
BIBLICAL REFERENCE: Psalm 150: 3-5; II Samuel 6: 6-19
MAJOR COLORS: browns and whites

JESUS RISES TRIUMPHANT FROM THE TOMB

LOCATION: Wesley Memorial Church, Oxford, England
INSTALLED: 1878
BIBLICAL REFERENCE: St. Mark 16: 9-15; St. Luke 24: 1-49;
St. John 20: 1-23; St. Matthew 28: 1-15
MAJOR COLORS: greens and yellows

GOD'S SPIRIT, AS A DOVE, ALIGHTS ON JESUS AT HIS BAPTISM

LOCATION: The Church of St. John, Gouda, Netherlands
INSTALLED: 1555
BIBLICAL REFERENCE: St. Matthew 3: 13-17; St. Mark 1: 9-11;
                    St. Luke 3: 21-22; St. John 1: 31-34
MAJOR COLORS: browns and yellows

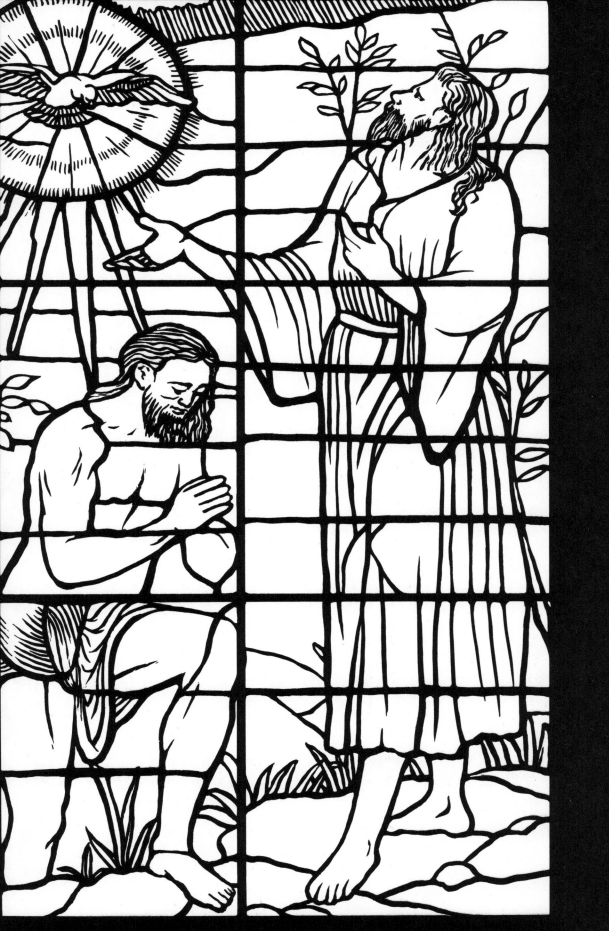

JESUS STANDS IN TRIAL BEFORE CAIAPHAS

LOCATION: Riverside Church, New York, New York, U.S.A.
INSTALLED: 1930
BIBLICAL REFERENCE: St. John 18: 12-24
MAJOR COLORS: oranges and grays

ST. PAUL AND DAVID FORETELL FINAL WORLD CONFLICTS

LOCATION: Cathedral Church of St. Peter and St. Paul,
Washington, D.C., U.S.A.

INSTALLED: 1935

BIBLICAL REFERENCE: II Samuel 23: 1-7; II Timothy 3: 1-14

MAJOR COLORS: greens and yellows

THE GOSPEL WRITERS, OR EVANGELISTS, COMMUNICATE THE
WORD OF GOD

LOCATION: St. Joan of Arc Church, La Place, Louisiana, U.S.A.
INSTALLED: 1988
BIBLICAL REFERENCE: St. Matthew 1: 1; St. Mark 1: 1; St. Luke 1: 1-14;
St. John 1: 1 and 21: 24-25; Revelation 4: 6-9
MAJOR COLORS: blues and greens

THE MOTHER OF JESUS RECEIVES A CROWN OF HEAVEN

LOCATION: St. Matthew the Apostle Church,
　　　　　River Ridge, New Orleans, Louisiana, U.S.A.

INSTALLED: 1985

BIBLICAL REFERENCE: St. Luke 1: 28-55; St. Matthew 1: 18-23;
　　　　　St. John 19: 25-27

MAJOR COLORS: golds and reds

ST. STEPHEN, THE FIRST MARTYR, STONED FOR HIS FAITH IN CHRIST

LOCATION: St. Paul's Episcopal Church, New Orleans, Louisiana, U.S.A.
INSTALLED: 1851
BIBLICAL REFERENCE: Acts 6: 1 through 8: 3
MAJOR COLORS: yellows and greens

ARCHANGELS MICHAEL AND GABRIEL ACT AS AGENTS FOR GOD

LOCATION: First Presbyterian Church,
          New Orleans, Louisiana, U.S.A.
INSTALLED: 1938
BIBLICAL REFERENCE: Revelation 12: 7; Jude 9; St. Luke 1: 26-38
MAJOR COLORS: greens and whites

EDITOR'S NOTE: All references are from the Authorized King James Version of the Bible.
Wherever necessary, design of the windows has been freely adapted for clarity and easier coloring.

LITTLE SIMON, Simon & Schuster Building, Rockefeller Center, 1230 Avenue of the Americas, New York, New York 10020. Illustrations
Copyright © 1990 by Ruth Goliwas. Text Copyright © 1990 by William H. Mackenzie Mackintosh. All rights reserved including the
right of reproduction in whole or in part in any form. LITTLE SIMON and colophon are trademarks of Simon & Schuster Inc.
Manufactured in the United States of America
10 9 8 7 6 5 4 3 2 1
ISBN: 0-671-69477-4